# 100 Practical Tips for Buying and Selling Real Estate

## Patricia O'Connor

# About the Author

Pat O'Connor is a licensed Florida real estate broker, instructor, and owner of The Veritas Real Estate Group, Inc., which she founded in 2004 in Fort Lauderdale. She was also a licensed Florida mortgage broker for seven years. Her company is a licensed real estate school as well as a brokerage firm, and she regularly teaches the Florida Sales Associate Pre-Licensing course at her office. Her real estate transactions include both residential and commercial properties in South Florida.

Prior to relocating to Florida in 2002, Ms. O'Connor was employed as a Vice President of Technology at a number of financial firms in New York City including Lehman Brothers, Merrill Lynch and PaineWebber. She has been teaching adults and developing course material since 1985. She was an Adjunct Professor at Saint Peter's University in Jersey City, N.J. and an Instructor at Columbia University in New York City. Ms. O'Connor enjoys writing about real estate and financial topics and has extensive experience as a freelance writer. Use the following link to view her current list of published books: http://amazon.com/author/patriciaoconnor

# Table of Contents

## 4.    Buyer Concerns                                    39

Buyer issues are very different from seller issues and the 18 tips in Chapter 4 cover the basics. Read about the importance of your credit score and the loan pre-approval process. Learn efficient ways to identify and view desirable properties. Understand how to structure a strong offer and what you should do after your offer is accepted.

## 5.    Investor Concerns                                 55

Investment property usually involves tenants, so Chapter 5 includes 10 tips on finding appropriate properties, customizing leases, property management, tenant screening and subsidized housing. Let the government pay your tenant's rent!

## 6.    Distressed Property Concerns                      63

Chapter 6 includes 20 practical tips to keep in mind if you're interested in buying foreclosure property or participating in a short sale. This section includes a discussion of liens and their importance to auction bidders. Read about the procedure for bidding on an FHA foreclosure home and learn about short sales from seller and buyer perspectives.

## 7.    Financing Concerns                                83

All prospective buyers need to understand the basics of financing if they want to obtain a favorable mortgage loan. The eight tips in Chapter 7 cover the basic types of loans and the use of retirement funds for real estate down payments or cash purchases. This discussion includes an insightful overview of self-directed IRAs and 401(k)s. Small Business Administration loans for the purchase of commercial owner-occupied properties are also discussed.

Everyone wants to optimize profits and avoid fines, and Chapter 8 includes 10 tips for accomplishing these goals. The discussion covers possible tax consequences for forgiven mortgage debt, capital gains and losses, the value of depreciation, property exchanges, tax law for foreign sellers, the Fair Housing Act, the Americans with Disabilities Act and closing options.

# 1

## Licensee Concerns

Real estate practitioners vary in knowledge, skill, likability and ethical standards, and your goal as a prospective customer is to choose an individual who is strong in all these attributes. You don't want to work with someone you can't trust. This chapter discusses ways to help you increase the probability of finding a reputable real estate licensee with whom you can establish a productive working relationship.

### *Tip #1: Work With a Realtor*

State laws don't require real estate licensees to join the National Association of Realtors (NAR); however, they do need to be a member and belong to a local Realtor association in order to have their own login to the Multiple Listing Service (MLS), which is the primary source of residential listings in the United States. If you're buying or selling residential real estate, ask the agent if she is a Realtor. If not, keep looking.

On the other hand, agents list commercial properties on many alternative sites. Consequently, many commercial real estate agents aren't Realtors because they don't need to access the MLS and have no desire to pay the Realtor fees.

Realtors are required to take ethics classes upon joining a Realtor association and every four years thereafter. Although unethical behavior is not necessarily illegal, it's not conducive to establishing a good working relationship with the public or other licensees. At the very least, the quadrennial classes remind the Realtors of the standards they should be striving to uphold. An ethics committee at the local association hears complaints against a Realtor, and may fine or sanction the licensee if it finds him guilty of violations. Members of the public should report illegal activity to the state's real estate commission.

### *Tip #2: Think Twice Before Working With a New Licensee*

This is painful for me to say, but you want to work with experienced sales people. Everybody has to start somewhere, but you don't want to be anyone's guinea pig. I started in the business in 2003, and I still learn something new in every transaction. Most new agents aren't yet aware of how much they don't know. They need to be able to price a property, advise a seller on staging techniques, understand and explain listing and sales contracts (particularly in states that don't require the use of an attorney), negotiate offers, track deadlines, keep their cool under trying circumstances, understand property taxes and know something about mortgage financing. Pre-licensing classes don't cover this material; it takes time to learn it all, and the new licensee already has his hands full learning how to find prospects.

### *Tip #3. Find an Agent*

Ask your friends, neighbors and family members if they can recommend a good agent. Word-of-mouth is an excellent way to find a qualified person. Once someone has been in the real estate business for a few years, much of her income is likely to come from repeat customers and referrals from previous customers.

You can also drive around your neighborhood and make a note of whose For Sale signs are posted in the front yards. Call a few of them and ask them to meet with you for an interview. Pick the one that suits you best. A preliminary interview happens more often with sellers rather than buyers because buyers typically first meet the agent at a prospective property. Unless you sign an agreement to work with that particular licensee, there's no penalty for choosing another person to show you properties if you're not happy with an agent.

Walk into a real estate office and talk to the on-site personnel. If you establish rapport with anyone in particular, then you can ask him about the possibility of working together.

Search the Internet for agents or listings in your city or subdivision. Be aware that many properties are advertised by multiple agents; it doesn't necessarily mean it's their listing just because it's featured on their website. That's OK. That's the way the business works. A Realtor can show you any property that's listed in her MLS.

### *Tip #4. Stay With an Agent You Like*

You don't need to keep contacting whoever advertises a property when you've already found another agent you trust. However, if you haven't narrowed down your search area, and potential homes are more than 10 miles apart, you might want to consider using multiple agents who are the most familiar with their own home turf. On the other hand, since it's so easy to find online listings, you're probably better off driving around neighborhoods and narrowing your search area before you ever start going inside homes.

### *Tip #5. Verify Licensing Status*

States provide a way for the public to verify the status of a licensee. Enter "< your state> real estate commission" and follow the links to verify if an individual is licensed. Because some agents may use nicknames on their business cards, you might have to look up the company first and then check what agents are listed under that company name.

### Tip #6. Report Illegal Activity

Engaging in unlicensed real estate activity for payment is a felony in many states, and you should immediately report these unscrupulous people to your state's real estate commission because they are a danger to the public. The only individuals who are allowed to receive compensation for showing you through a property or assisting you with leasing a property are licensed real estate professionals. One exception is a salaried employee who is showing property as part of their job description, and who is not paid a commission or a bonus based on the outcome of the transaction.

### Tip #7. Make an Appointment

If you want to receive the best service, make an appointment to meet with an agent and preferably give them 24 hours' notice. Agents need time to determine the market value of your home before a listing appointment, and they may have to wait for confirmation from listing agents before they can show you a property. This is particularly true if you want to look at properties over the weekend. It's often difficult to reach listing agents on Friday nights, Saturdays, and Sunday mornings. If you know you want to look at something on a Saturday afternoon, play it safe and let the agent know on Friday morning. You'll have fewer disappointments if you can plan ahead.

If you're interested in viewing commercial properties, be aware that many commercial real estate agents don't work on weekends, so plan accordingly.

### *Tip #8. Don't Pay Real Estate Processing Fees*

As the value of homes decrease, the number of real estate agents charging buyers and sellers extra fees increases. In most cases, this is a total rip-off by greedy agents and brokers. Unless they are going above and beyond what is normally expected to earn a commission, don't pay them a dime extra. It's a disgraceful practice.

Mortgage companies legitimately charge a processing fee because there are usually reams of paperwork and hours of follow-up involved in obtaining a mortgage loan approval. In addition, it's the processor who may be speaking with the loan underwriter and the applicant to resolve open issues.

This is not the case in real estate transactions. Some companies hire closing coordinators to ensure that the process is a smooth one. However, there are usually very few benchmarks to track in a residential transaction. Deadlines that need watching include completion of home inspections, deliverance of association documents, property appraisal, loan application, loan approval and closing date. If you pay cash, that eliminates three of the items; you won't need an appraisal, loan application or loan approval. Is this task worth hundreds of dollars out of your own pocket? Shouldn't this be the job of the listing agent? If the brokerage firm wants to provide assistance to the listing agent, that's fine and dandy but why the heck are you paying for it? It's their job!

The one exception that comes to mind is a short sale. The seller typically has no closing costs, so in those cases when the lender refuses to pay for the seller's attorney or other fees, it's a common practice to ask the buyer to pay the fees. If they refuse, either the real estate agents pay them or the deal falls apart.

I have even seen listing agents trying to charge *buyers* a fee for storing documents. The fees are stated in the MLS and go as high as $495. This usually happens with the non-franchised brokerage firms. If you are a fed-up agent, report these agents immediately to your state's real estate commission as a possible violation of the Real Estate Settlement Procedures Act (RESPA). If the state gets enough complaints, maybe they'll act to stop the practice. If they don't act, contact the U.S. Department of Housing and Urban Development (HUD), which enforces RESPA.

What do you think? If you are looking for a straight-shooting agent, send me an email at poconnor@

veritasrealestategroup.com with the subject line "Help Me Find an Agent," and I will do my best to find you someone in your area who doesn't charge extra fees.

If you're a real estate agent that doesn't charge a processing fee, send me an email at poconnor@ veritasrealestategroup.com with the subject line "Available Agent." Let me know the area you serve, and I will add you to my database of referral agents.

# 2

## Contractual Concerns

Real estate transactions are seldom sealed with a handshake. In today's litigious society, your interests are best served when you sign a legally binding document that clearly states the responsibilities of all the parties. Sellers sign a listing agreement, perhaps a seller's property disclosure and the offer; buyers sign the offer, perhaps a buyer/broker agreement, seller's property disclosure and a stack of mortgage loan documents if they are financing the purchase. These documents are important so make sure that you understand what you're signing.

### *Tip #9. Read Everything Before You Sign Anything*

If you're like most people, your eyes start to blur and your mind wanders when you try to read a legal contract. There is so much "legalese" in many of the agreements that your head starts to spin. Nevertheless, you need to read and understand everything you're signing. Don't count on your real estate agent to explain it to you; he may not completely understand it himself. For residential transactions, the agents are most likely using standard contracts provided by the state's Realtor Association. The agent may know how to fill in the blanks, but there may be pages of additional information that aren't as clearly understood.

If you're selling a residential property, ask your agent to email you blank sample contracts so that you can start reading them before you receive an offer. If you're a buyer, request a blank copy when you first start your search.

### *Tip #10. Use an Attorney*

Some states require that attorneys represent both buyers and sellers of real estate. Other states have no such regulation. If you choose legal representation, make sure that you work with an experienced real estate attorney and not a criminal defense or divorce attorney.

If you have an attorney, keep her in the loop during the negotiations and throughout the process. Have her approve any contract changes before you sign anything. Send her copies of every document related to the deal. You want her legal oversight on all agreements and not just for the closing settlement.

At that point, it's probably too late to modify any unfavorable terms.

While your state may not mandate the use of an attorney, you should always use one if you are buying a bank-owned foreclosure property. You may make your offer on a standard Realtor Association contract, but the lender will probably include a multi-page addendum that states the addendum takes precedence over the other contract if there's a conflict. I have seen addenda that were 14 pages long, and they are always written to favor the lender. Have an attorney review it and handle any negotiated changes to the document.

Option contracts are another example of a document that an attorney should review. Real estate agents aren't usually as familiar with them, and the wording in options is particularly tricky. There can be plenty of room for one party or another to wiggle out of the agreement if they are not correctly written. For example, if you are looking to lease with an option to purchase, absolutely have a real estate attorney review the option before you submit the offer. Likewise, sellers should have an attorney review any submitted options.

### *Tip #11. Understand Your Legal Rights*

If you don't understand something, ask your real estate agent or attorney. Real estate agents prefer that you ask an attorney in many circumstances because they are not allowed to give a legal opinion, and some of your questions may require one.

When you apply for a loan, you'll be asked to sign a number of documents. Be sure that you understand what you are signing. Realize that the lender can make a claim on your property and possibly evict you if you fall behind in your mortgage payments. You can also lose your home if you don't pay your property tax or association maintenance fees.

### *Tip #12. Negotiate the Listing Agreement*

Almost everything in real estate is negotiable including the seller's listing agreement with a real estate broker. This tip might make a lot of agents mad at me, but I am writing this for the consumer and not for the commission-driven professionals.

Six months is a reasonable listing time for most residential properties; commercial listings may be longer. If the house doesn't sell within this timeframe, you have a choice of renewing the agreement or finding another agent. If the residential agent insists on a 12-month term, contact someone else. If you're bound to 12 months and the agent doesn't do anything to promote your property, you may have to pay a hefty cancellation fee if you want to prematurely terminate the contract.

The cancellation fee may be a stated dollar amount or a percentage of the list price. If you feel that it is extreme, try to negotiate it down. You never know what circumstances may force you to cancel the sale. Once again, if you don't like the terms, it won't hurt to shop around and interview other agents. However, not all real estate agents are created equal. If your agent comes highly recommended, or you have successfully done business with her in the past, think twice before switching to someone else.

Conversations about the amount of the real estate sales commission are the least favorite thing agents want to discuss. They usually split the commission with their broker, and that split may be 50/50 for a new agent. Most agents receive no salary, bonus or benefits. Their share of the commission may be the only income they have to support an entire family.

By federal law, commissions are negotiable. However, the listing agent's broker may set the minimum amount she will accept. If you're an investor who buys and sells a number of properties using this agent, or you're also using your listing agent to find you a new home to purchase, you have more leverage for a commission reduction. In addition, you may have some luck negotiating a reduction in commission if your listing agent also finds the buyer for your property. In this case, a one-percent reduction in commission is likely to be acceptable.

In the U.S., the seller typically pays the full commission for both the seller's and buyer's residential real estate agent. In commercial transactions, it is common for the sellers to only pay the listing agent. However, if the property is listed for sale in the MLS, the seller must agree to pay the buyer's agent something.

### *Tip #13. Understand the Buyer Broker Agreement*

If the seller isn't paying the buyer's agent, the only alternative is for the buyer to pay it; otherwise, the agent is working for free. The buyer broker agreement comes in many forms, but basically, it's used to contractually obligate the buyer to pay all or part of his agent's commission if it is not being paid by the seller.

The agreement may also require the buyer to use the services of only one agent for a specified period of time. If the buyer uses someone else and closes a transaction within that timeframe, the buyer will owe the commission to the agent with the signed agreement. If the buyer imprudently signs multiple buyer broker agreements with various agents, he may find himself on the hook for paying commissions to a number of different agents. Read everything before you sign it.

### *Tip #14. Know the Purchase Contract Contingencies*

Just because everyone has signed the purchase agreement, it doesn't mean the deal will close. Most contracts allow the buyer to cancel if problems are discovered during the home inspection, if the appraisal value is less than the accepted sales price or if the buyer is unable to obtain a mortgage loan.

However, in a red-hot real estate market, the listing agent may require that the buyers waive the appraisal contingency. Licensees do this when there aren't many homes listed for sale, and prospective buyers have to bid against each other for the home. These homes frequently sell for more than the list price and more than the current market value of the neighborhood. The listing agent knows this and requires that any submitted offers exclude the condition that the buyer can cancel if the property appraises below the accepted offer price. In a case like this, the lender only lends money based on the appraisal value, and the buyer has to pay the difference in cash at the closing.

For simplicity's sake, let's assume the lender has agreed to 100 percent financing. The accepted offer price is $200,000, but the appraisal value is $180,000. If the seller doesn't agree to lower the sale price, the buyer must pay the $20,000 difference ($200,000 minus $180,000) out of his own pocket at the closing if the appraisal contingency was waived. If it wasn't waived, the buyer can walk away from the deal and recover the earnest money deposit.

If a property needs repairs, the listing agent may require only cash offers because he knows that lenders may not want to finance the purchase of damaged properties. This doesn't mean the property is worthless. Handymen search high and low for properties they can renovate, and the listing agent may receive multiple cash offers.

Discuss market conditions with your real estate agent and how it affects list price, offers and days on market (the number of days a property is listed before there's an accepted offer).

## *Tip #15. Don't Lose Your Earnest Money Deposit*

The best advice I can give you is to stay committed to your agreements and don't risk losing your earnest money deposit. Keep an open mind and allow your real estate agent or attorney to try to work out a compromise for issues before matters escalate beyond the point where the deal is no longer salvageable. Remember, almost everything in real estate transactions is negotiable if people remain civil.

Even though the contract states you have the right to cancel under certain circumstances, you might have to go to court to have your good faith money returned to you. In some cases, if the real estate broker is holding the escrow money in his own trust account, the money can be returned immediately if the broker has no doubts about who is entitled to the money. Otherwise, the parties may decide to sue each other if they don't agree to let an arbitrator decide the case for them. An arbitrator is someone who hears the evidence outside of a courtroom and makes a binding ruling. Judge Judy is a popular example of a former judge who became an arbitrator and television personality.

If a title company or attorney has the escrow money, both the buyer and seller have to agree to release the money to the party who wishes to cancel. If that's not possible and they can't work out a compromise, a lawsuit may be the only solution.

If the seller signs the contract and then changes her mind about moving, bad things can happen. A judge may find that she is in breach of contract and order her to sell the house to the buyer and pay all the buyer's court costs and attorney's fees.

Homeowner's remorse is a common condition in which buyers start to second-guess themselves shortly after they sign an offer. If their doubts are strong enough, they may attempt to get out of the contract. With this in mind, they may not try very hard to find financing and stop looking if one lender denies their loan application. The seller may think they should have applied to a more flexible second lender. The broker has doubts about the buyer's good faith, and trouble ensues. Both parties may sue each other for the money, and the case could take months to be resolved.

### *Tip #16.  Hire a Home Inspector for As-Is Purchase Contract*

An as-is purchase contract is usually used when a seller doesn't want to be required to pay a certain amount toward repairs; it doesn't mean repair costs can't be negotiated if the home inspector uncovers some major problems. A "normal" purchase contract states that the seller will contribute a specified amount of money toward the repair of serious problems. An as-is contract has no such provision. That's the main difference between the two types of contracts. Unfortunately, many buyers and their real estate agents don't understand this, and the buyer may not even bother to have a home inspection because he is under the delusion that he has to accept the property no matter what its condition if it is an as-is contract. This is wrong, wrong, wrong. Always have a home inspection, or you may end up having to pay thousands of dollars to fix roofing, plumbing or electrical problems.

### *Tip #17. Pay Attention to Contract Dates*

Dates on the contract are more than just suggestions. For example, if the purchase contract gives you ten days after offer acceptance to have a home inspection and notify the seller of needed repairs, you shouldn't wait two weeks to order the home inspection. By doing so, you may have lost your right to cancel the contract if the inspection uncovers evidence of serious damage.

Some contracts state that time is of the essence. This is strong legal language that reinforces the idea that a missed contractual date constitutes a material breach of contract. A purchase contract normally has a number of deadlines including timeframes for the home inspection, loan application, loan approval and the closing date.

Suppose the buyer isn't ready to close on time, and the seller has received a better offer and refuses to sign an addendum to extend the closing date. The seller says that it's a dead deal while the buyer claims he was acting in good faith and files a lawsuit against the seller. How will this end? Well, for starters, the attorneys will be a little richer, and the buyer and seller will be a little poorer. Whether or not a judge will find the delaying party is in breach of the contract depends on the individual circumstances and local custom. Try to avoid putting yourself in a situation that may result in court action and pay attention to the dates.

### *Tip #18. Address Post-Closing Problems Quickly*

Imagine that you just moved into your new home, and your roof leaks during the first rainstorm. Do you think you might be a little upset? Maybe more than a little angry? Maybe furious? That's OK; you have a right to be mad. Once you cool off a bit, call your real estate agent and explain the situation. Ask her if she knew about any problems with the roof. If she denies any knowledge of the fact, ask her to get the phone number of the seller. Contact a roofer and ask him for a repair estimate; then call the seller, and ask him to pay for the roof repair. If he refuses, be prepared to hire an attorney.

State law requires that sellers disclose any known latent defects in the home before the parties finalize the contract. Latent defects are issues that aren't obvious to someone walking through a home, but materially affect the value of the property. It includes broken appliances, broken floor tiling underneath an area rug, cracks in the foundation, plumbing and electrical problems and roofing problems. It doesn't include broken windows, missing screens, chipped bathtubs or torn wallpaper; this damage is visible and not hidden from sight. This disclosure requirement applies even if you have an as-is contract, and it is not waived if you hire a home inspector.

If you believe that the seller and/or real estate agent deliberately withheld damaging information, contact a real estate attorney as soon as possible after you discover the problem. States have limits on when you can file lawsuits involving written contracts. This is called the statute of limitations and varies among states; timeframes can be anywhere from three to ten years after closing.

A common judgment in cases like this is that the seller pays three times the cost of repairs as well as the buyer's attorney fees and court costs. Contact a real estate attorney for additional information if you believe you have a case. Be sure to keep all of your repair receipts and make notes on any discussions you have with the seller or real estate agent about the problem. Include the date and time of the meetings or phone calls. A paper trail will help your attorney prove your case.

The same advice holds true if you are a seller who believes that you are being unjustly accused. Keep notes about any interactions you have with the buyer, real estate agent or attorneys and hire your own real estate attorney.

# 3

---

## Seller Concerns

Sellers usually want to maximize their profits and sell the property as quickly as possible. Here are some tips to help you achieve that goal.

### *Tip #19. Make Cost-Effective Home Improvements*

People deserve to be comfortable where they live, and one of the joys of buying your own home is your right to do pretty much whatever you want with it. You can knock down walls or build a pool and as long as the work is properly permitted, nobody will say a thing. However, don't expect to recoup all of your investment when you're ready to sell the home.

For example, you may have a beautiful saltwater infinity pool with a grotto and waterfall that cost $40,000 to construct. You have enjoyed many hours of relaxation in that pool and feel that the money was well spent. Prospective buyers, on the other hand, may feel differently and, in some neighborhoods, the pool may add nothing to the appraisal value of the home.

Perhaps you really like marble bathrooms and flooring, but you live in a neighborhood where the value of the surrounding homes doesn't support such an expense. Go ahead and install it if that's what you want, but a buyer may not pay any more for this than he would pay for the neighbor's home with tile floors. This is called an over-improvement; a condition that occurs when the remodeling is more expensive than the neighborhood warrants and consequently, doesn't significantly increase the market value of the home.

Remodeled kitchens and master bathrooms are the two rooms that get the most attention from the buyers, and the return on your investment is likely to be highest in these areas. At the very least, make sure the woodwork in these rooms is clean and in good repair and that the walls look freshly painted or wallpapered.

### *Tip #20. Hire a Home Inspector*

Hire a home inspector and make needed repairs before you list the home if you want to limit the possibility of losing good buyers. If you don't have the money to fix problems, disclose known issues to prospective buyers and price the home accordingly. You might ask the listing agent to accept only as-is offers and mark it in the MLS as a "handyman special" type of property.

That helps ensure you will attract the type of buyers who are willing to fix the problems themselves.

### Tip #21. Disclose Latent Defects

A latent defect is something that's not obvious to the casual observer and that materially affects the value of the property. Once you're aware of something, state laws require that you disclose it to potential buyers. Some states require written disclosure while others are satisfied with verbal notification. Specific disclosure requirements vary between states, and it may be illegal to disclose the medical condition of occupants or former occupants in your state. Some states require disclosure of known murders or suicides that occurred on the property, but other states don't have such a requirement. Common disclosures include roof or plumbing leaks, electrical problems, cracks in the foundation and liens on the property. Your listing agent will most likely have you complete a state-approved disclosure form to protect you as well as her. Complete this to the best of your ability even if it is an investment property where you didn't personally reside. You still know about the major repairs because you paid for them.

### Tip #22. Insist on MLS Listing

Some real estate brokers offer to list the property for a lower amount of sales commission if the seller agrees not to have the property listed in the MLS. This is called a pocket listing, and I believe it is bad for the seller and the cooperative real estate industry. The broker is trying to guarantee that his office will be paid the entire commission without having to split it with a buyer's broker.

In my opinion, properties with the most visibility will sell for the highest price in the shortest amount of time. If nobody knows that your property is for sale except the agents within a particular office or franchise, you are operating at a distinct disadvantage. You won't have the same number of showings that an MLS listing generates and there's a more limited opportunity for buyers to engage in a bidding war during a seller's market. Think twice before signing such an agreement and question the motives of the agent who may be trying to convince you that it's in your best interest to limit exposure.

## Tip #23. Pay Attention to the Showing Instructions

Read the showing instruction section of the listing agreement very carefully because it affects your safety and the safety of your valuables. There are basically four ways that real estate agents gain access to a property in order to show it. The front door key is placed in a compartment inside a combination lockbox; the key is placed in an electronic lockbox that can only be opened by someone with a Realtor-issued transponder; the listing agent is in the home during all the showings; or the owner lets the prospects and their agent into the home.

All of these methods are commonly used, but you do not want a combination lockbox on your door! This is a very dangerous practice because the seller doesn't know who has been given the lock's combination. Some real estate agents are too lazy to get off their duff, and they tell prospective buyers the combination and ask them to go look at it by themselves. Other agents actually put the combination code in the MLS listing, which may be visible to the public. Still others may mention the code as they are opening the lockbox, which allows the buyer to revisit the property without an agent. Even well-meaning agents can give out the code. Suppose the listing agent is driving and receives a call asking for showing instructions. The agent assumes it is another Realtor and gives the unknown caller the combination. Limit your chance of a robbery or personal injury and don't allow the listing agent to use a combination lockbox.

An electronic lockbox is safer because Realtors are the only ones who can purchase a transponder that opens the box, and they can only purchase one. However, lazy and uncaring agents can give buyers the gadget and tell them to go to the property by themselves. But, the name of the transponder's Realtor owner is recorded every time an electronic lockbox is accessed, so if anything does happen, at least you know the agent who allowed people access to the home.

If you're worried about your things, you can insist that the listing agent be present in the home during all the showings, and you can occasionally stay home yourself.

Some overly eager prospective buyers like to walk around the yard and peep in the windows of homes they might like to see. To help prevent this from happening, sellers might not want a For Sale sign in the yard and may request that a lockbox is placed out of sight and not hanging from the front doorknob. This will keep people from stopping and investigating when they just happen to be driving by and notice a For Sale sign.

### *Tip #24. Consider Including Furniture*

If you're not planning to take the furniture with you when you move, ask the listing agent to list the property as partially furnished or furniture negotiable. This may increase the number of people who want to see the property, and your agent might use some of the furniture as a negotiation tool after the home inspection. Suppose the buyers requested $2,000 for repairs. They might be willing to accept some of the furniture in lieu of payment. It's a win-win for everybody. You get paid for some of the furniture, and the buyers appreciate the gesture. This is particularly true in as-is contracts where the sellers aren't required to pay a stated amount toward repairs.

## Tip #25. Offer a Service Warranty

Older appliances turn off many prospective buyers.
To help alleviate fears of endless repair bills, offer
a service warranty that covers the cost of repair
or replacement of major appliances including the
refrigerator, stove, dishwasher, washer and dryer. If the
central air conditioning is also old, sellers can cover
that as well. Plans may be available for less than $400.
Ask your listing agent to include the warranty offer in
the listing information.

## Tip #26. Mention Government Loans

If you currently have an outstanding FHA, VA or
USDA mortgage loan, mention this fact to your
listing agent. These loans are assumable by qualified
borrowers and might be a great selling point if the
interest rate is lower than the prevailing interest rate.
You want to make sure that the agent mentions this
in the listing because it will attract buyers who can
assume the loan at the same terms, including the low
interest rate.

## Tip #27. Consider Seller Financing

If you're selling your home and have no mortgage to
pay off, you might want to consider seller financing
in which you provide a mortgage loan for a buyer
who is unable or who doesn't wish to obtain a loan

from a traditional lender. In addition to a sizable down payment, the buyer would make monthly mortgage payments to you at an interest rate that is higher than what the lenders are currently charging. Since you probably don't want this to continue for 15 or 30 years, you might require a 3-or 5-year balloon mortgage.

In a balloon mortgage, the lender calculates the monthly payment as if it was going to continue for 30 years, but it requires a lump sum payoff after a much shorter time. Hopefully, during this time, the buyer can improve his own situation, refinance with a traditional lender and pay you the loan balance when it's due; otherwise, he will have to find the cash. If neither one of these options is possible, you can foreclose and evict him for defaulting on the mortgage. The house is back in your hands, and you can sell it again. Discuss this with a real estate attorney if the idea seems right for your situation. It can be a viable solution if you are trying to sell a home when credit is tight, and you don't live in an area with many cash buyers.

### *Tip #28. Allow Other Agents to Advertise Listing*

In most cases, it's to the seller's advantage to obtain as much advertising exposure as possible. Let other agents advertise your property in newspapers and on their websites. Why not? Listing agents may not want you to allow it because they may want less exposure to increase the chance that they will find a buyer and earn both sides of the commission. Unless the listing agent offers a believable and compelling argument for limiting the amount of exposure, permit it.

### Tip #29. Request an Emailed Copy of the MLS Listing

Ask your agent to email you a copy of the listing once it's published so you can check it for accuracy and impact. If the photographs are poor, ask her to replace them with better shots. Don't be shy; you are paying her a sales commission with the expectation that she does a good job. You should also request a copy of any advertising that she publishes on your behalf.

### Tip #30. Ask for Weekly Updates

Let your listing agent know from day one that you expect a weekly update on showing and advertising activity. The report should include the number of showings, feedback from the buyers, any tentative offers, repeat showings and marketing efforts. Be prepared for the fact that most of the activity usually occurs within the first two weeks of listing the property. If showings slow to a crawl, consider lowering the asking price and increasing the advertising.

## *Tip #31. Prepare the House for Optimal Showings*

Don't ask your listing agent to clean the house for you if you're an absentee owner. Either clean it yourself or let your agent hire a professional cleaning service to do the job. If the agent does it, she will resent you, and the home isn't going to sparkle the way it should. This is not one of the areas where you want to try and save money. A clean house will sell faster than a dirty one. Don't forget to clean the carpets.

Prospective buyers want to be able to envision themselves living in the home as they walk through the rooms. Remove personal items from tabletops and clear off the kitchen counters. Store the toaster, blender and coffee maker somewhere else. If it's February and the Christmas tree is still up, take it down. Store some of the furniture in the basement if doing so makes the room look bigger. Do you really need that extra loveseat or overstuffed chair? If the place looks better without it, remove it. Hire a professional stager if you can't make any headway on your own.

The front of the house is the first thing that anyone sees so make it welcoming. Put a fresh coat of paint or varnish on the door if it's looking a little worn and replace a wooden threshold with a metal strip if there's sign of wood rot. Plant flowers near the doorway if the season permits and make sure that the shrubs are trimmed, and the grass is cut. First impressions are very important, and the outward appearance is often an accurate indicator of the interior condition.

A home appears more welcoming when the lights are on, even in the middle of the day. If you know ahead of time that a showing is scheduled, make sure that every room, including the bathroom, is lit before you leave the house. Many buyer's agents will do this if it's not already done, but don't rely on them.

Clean the windows and open the blinds. Let the sun shine through and fill the home with a warm glow. Oftentimes, a pleasant view will seal the deal.

Don't delude yourself into thinking that everyone who walks into your home is an honest individual. While they may not break into a home and rob it, a crime of opportunity may be too tempting to resist. Hide your jewelry, watches and money somewhere other than your dresser drawer. It's easy enough for a thief to open a drawer while the agent is talking to someone else in another room. Likewise, take prescription drugs out of the medicine cabinet and place them in a less conspicuous area.

People entering a home for the first time are going to notice odors more than the people that live there. Make sure the litter box is clean and remove any doggie smell from the furniture. Open the windows and air out the rooms if the weather permits. Buy some flowers and have them displayed on the dining room table.

Scents like orange, lemon, pine and vanilla are clean smells that don't overwhelm the senses.

If you're a smoker, refrain from lighting up inside the home until the sale closes. Studies have shown that homes with smokers typically sell for significantly less money than non-smoker's homes. You may not smell it anymore, but everybody else does.

### *Tip #32. Leave the Home*

Common wisdom says that buyers feel more comfortable in a home when the owners aren't there. They are more apt to open the closet doors and spend time taking pictures and videos if someone isn't following them around the house. Even if the owner remains in one room, the buyers may feel too inhibited to talk about what they like or dislike about different features. They don't want to appear rude, so they don't discuss their preferences. This makes the place more forgettable and prevents the buyer's agent from helping to sell the home. It's harder to talk about the great view or inviting jacuzzi if the buyers aren't feeling comfortable. Do yourself a favor and go for a walk around the neighborhood during the showing.

### *Tip #33. Don't Allow Public Open Houses*

There are two types of open houses. One is for other real estate agents and gives them a chance to preview a home so that they can recommend it to potential buyers. The listing agent may arrange for a catered buffet lunch, and alcohol might be included. The listing agent will ask for feedback on the appearance of the home and whether or not the other professionals feel that it is priced correctly. In some cities, the listing agents coordinate these broker's showings so that they are held on the same day of the week. This gives the interested agents a chance to preview multiple homes in a single day and is a productive use of everyone's time.

The other type of open house is one in which the listing agent sits alone waiting for strangers to come in. She may have tied balloons to the mailbox and have an Open House sign in the yard. If she's smart, she also has a registration form by the front door and asks everyone who enters to write down his name, phone number and email. Some of the information will be bogus, but it's a source of buyer leads for the agent, and this is the prime reason why she is having the open house in the first place. Most homes don't sell because of an open house. The neighbors come in to see it and casual buyers may ask questions, but most buyers search on the Internet and make an appointment with a Realtor to see a property.

As a seller, you have no idea who may stop by. If there's a large group of people at any one time, the listing agent can't stay close to all of them. People could be rifling through your drawers, checking out your security system or going through your medicine cabinet. The risks outweigh the benefits, in my opinion.

### *Tip #34. Keep the Water On*

When no one is living in a home, there's a temptation to save money by canceling the water account. Unfortunately, this plan doesn't work when it comes time to show the property. Inevitably, some people want to use the bathroom facilities when nature calls, and they are in a house. Either they won't check to see if the water is on or the need is too great to wait, and the listing agent ends up having to deal with an unflushed toilet. If the buyer's agent fails to mention this condition to the listing agent after a showing, the mess may not be remedied for days or weeks. It goes without saying that this type of situation has an adverse effect on buyers.

Another reason for leaving the water on is to prevent sewer gases from coming up through the pipes. If water isn't run, the pipes under the sinks and toilets dry out, a valve loses its seal and opens, and methane gas enters the house from the sewer lines. Make sure your listing agent knows this and ask her to occasionally run the water in the sinks and flush the toilets if the property is going to be vacant for an extended period of time.

# 4

---

## Buyer Concerns

Buying real estate is one of the most expensive purchases most people ever make. It can also be one of the more stressful situations in someone's life. This is particularly true for a first-time buyer who has not yet experienced the joys and pitfalls of trying to find the right house. That individual will have a rougher time than the professional investor who makes a living buying properties. Practice makes perfect, and subsequent purchases should be easier than the first. Hopefully, these tips will help smooth the process for you.

### *Tip #35. Check Your Credit Report*

If you are planning to apply for a mortgage loan, check your credit report when you first start thinking about the possibility of buying a home. Your credit score has a significant impact on your ability to be approved for a loan.

Identity theft is epidemic, and you may not know if someone else is masquerading as you unless you check the report. Broken romantic relationships often cause one partner to seek revenge by going on a shopping spree with the ex's credit card. While you may be able to straighten this out with the creditor, it will take time.

Paying cash for everything is a prudent way to manage your finances, but it's not helping your credit score. If you don't have any credit cards or car payments, apply for three cards. You can pay off the balance every month so that you're not incurring interest fees, but you need to use the cards. Lenders want to see three lines of credit with no late payments. If possible, start using the cards a year in advance of your anticipated purchase so that you establish a strong credit history before you apply for a mortgage loan.

Credit scores are partially based on the ratio between used credit and available credit limits. Therefore, when you're applying for a new credit card ask for a high credit limit and keep the balance owed at 75 percent below that limit. If you already have credit cards, call customer service and try to increase the available limit and pay down the card so that you have a 75 percent available credit line. These practices should go a long way toward improving your credit score.

If you recently went through financially rough times and suffered through late mortgage payments, a foreclosure or a bankruptcy, your credit score is going to be adversely affected, and you may not qualify for a new traditional credit card. If you find yourself in this situation, try applying for a secured credit card in which the consumer deposits money in a lender's account, and this amount becomes the basis for the card's credit limit. Credit score isn't important, but your amount of debt and income is. You have to have enough discretionary income to make the monthly card payments. The payment history for a secured credit card appears on the credit report and can increase your credit score if you make the payments on time. Remember, the larger the amount of available credit, the better.

### *Tip #36. Save Your Money*

Many potential homebuyers underestimate the amount of money they'll need to purchase a home, even if they're approved for a loan. For starters, lenders require verification that you have at least enough money in the bank to make two months of mortgage payments after the closing.

In addition, most sellers require proof of a buyer's good intentions in the form of a cash deposit that is held in a trust account by your real estate broker, attorney or title company. The amount of this good faith money (also called earnest money) depends on what the seller wants and local convention. In many parts of the country, financed borrowers will need to submit 3-to-5 percent of the offer price, and cash buyers will need 10 percent. It's not a legal requirement, but the seller probably won't accept your offer without it. If the buyer cancels the contract without a legitimate legal reason for doing so, the buyer usually forfeits the money to the seller as compensation for taking the property off the market and losing other potential buyers. If the deal proceeds to closing, the escrowed money is applied toward the buyer's closing costs. The amount of good faith money has nothing at all to do with the type of loan and is not the same as a lender's down payment.

The amount of down payment that's required depends on the lender. Before the 2007 financial meltdown, many borrowers received 100 percent financing with no down payment. After the crash, lenders tightened their guidelines and most borrowers needed a five-percent minimum down payment. Two current exceptions are VA loans to qualified active military personnel and veterans, and USDA loans to rural, low-income individuals; both programs allow for 100 percent financing. In South Florida, if you want to purchase a condominium, you will probably need a 20-to-25 percent down payment. That's because so many of these units ended up in foreclosure that they are considered a high risk for lenders in this area. The situation can change as the economy and job markets improve, but that's the 2013 state of affairs.

Other charges also mount up. You will probably want a home inspection, and a lender requires a property appraisal. Home insurance companies require that you pay a year's premium in advance for coverage, so add that to your list of expenses. Title insurance is discussed later in the chapter, but that may be an additional cost, and you'll have to pay the loan officer for his time and effort.

The amount you'll need to pay for any of these services varies by your location; do an Internet search and look for local providers' websites. Property insurance costs can be vastly different between companies, so do your homework and choose wisely.

### *Tip #37. Get Pre-Approved*

Talk to a loan officer before you even start looking at homes. If you don't qualify for a mortgage, then there's no point wasting time driving around looking at properties, and perceptive real estate agents only work with buyers who are pre-approved. If you do qualify, the loan officer will tell you how much you can afford to pay for a home. With that information, you can start choosing particular neighborhoods.

The loan officer will counsel you on the steps you need to take for a future approval if you're turned down during your first visit. Don't get too discouraged. It could be that you have been working for only one year; most lenders require two years for approval. Your credit score might be a little too low; listen to the loan officer's advice on how to raise it enough to qualify for a loan. Just because you can't get a mortgage the first time you try, it doesn't mean you'll never get one.

## *Tip #38. Search the Internet*

Once you know your price range, start looking at properties that are listed for sale on the Internet. There are a large number of websites with listings that are grouped by state, city or subdivision. Conduct an Internet search and you will likely see pages of links. Realtor.com lists the properties that are in the MLS, and the status of each one is kept current. Some of your searches on other sites may list properties that sold two or more years ago.

## *Tip #39. Make a List*

Start making a list of the neighborhoods in your price range that you prefer. If you already live close by, drive around and see if the houses and yards are well maintained. Call the local police station and ask about the crime rate in any particular area. Get out of the car and talk to the neighbors. Ask them about association fees and if there's a community pool. Any potential playmates for your young children? How are the schools rated in this district? Gather as much information as possible ahead of time to help you make up your mind about a particular subdivision or condominium complex.

## *Tip #40. Work With a Realtor*

Realtors are ready, willing and able to help you find the perfect property, and it usually doesn't cost the buyer anything for their services. In the United States, the residential seller typically pays the commission for the seller's and buyer's agent. Let the agent know that you are already pre-approved for a loan or paying cash for the property. Most listing agents require the pre-approval letter or proof of cash funds to be submitted with the offer.

One way to find a home is for the buyer to search the Internet and email the Realtor the addresses or MLS numbers of the properties that look interesting. If that's not convenient, tell the agent the price range, neighborhood and important features that you desire including the number of bedrooms and baths, pool, garage, fenced-in yard, number of stories and view. If you're looking for a condo, remember to tell the agent if you have a pet, and if you need a washer and dryer in the unit. Many condo buildings have a community laundry room and don't allow washer and dryer hookups in the unit.

If you're meeting the agent at a property, please be on time. The Realtors are professionals and deserve to be treated in a professional manner.

## *Tip #41. Keep the Kids Home*

If the kids are in their running-around stage, keep them home when you are looking at property. There is too great a chance that they will damage something, and it's very hard for the adults to focus on the house if they have to keep an eye on the young ones.

In addition, don't bring your adorable dog to a showing. That should be an obvious thing; however, personal experience compels me to mention it. You can find out if Rover likes the place after you move in. He'll adjust; don't sweat it.

## *Tip #42. Take Videos or Pictures*

Creating your own visual tour is a great idea and can be done with most cellphones. You might even be able to stream the video to your partner at home who can serve as a director requesting close-ups and views from different angles.

The first shot in every video or photograph album should be of the property address, whether it's on the mailbox or the front of the home. This will help you keep the individual homes clearer in your mind when you review the pictures at a later date.

## *Tip #43. Limit the Number of Showings*

Unless you're coming to town for only one day, limit
the number of properties you see to a maximum of
five at a time. Allowing for driving time between
properties, this can easily take three or more hours.
A more manageable number for everyone involved is
three at a time. After that, many people begin to lose
focus, and the homes start to run together. If you're
feeling tired, don't be afraid to ask the agent to stop at
a fast-food place for coffee. She may even pay!

## *Tip #44. Keep an Open Mind*

Styles of homes display distinct regional differences.
In South Florida, concrete block homes are common
and serve as a defense against termites and hurricane-
force winds; you won't see a wood-framed three-
story colonial home anywhere in the area. If you're
relocating from another part of the country, you may
need to adjust your preferences or buy a condo unit.

Hopefully, the seller has cleaned the home prior to the
showing. However, this is not always the case. Try to
overlook the clutter and the grime. Keep in mind that
cosmetic problems are easily remedied. If you come
to a property wearing white gloves and swiping your
palm over any suspicious areas, you may be looking
for a place to buy for a long time. You can always hire
a cleaning service before you move in. Concentrate on
the features of the home.

In a seller's market, there may not be many homes
listed for sale, so you'll have fewer choices. Think
about your ability to add features that you want that
aren't already in place, and you may be able to broaden
your search criteria. For example, instead of just
looking at pool homes, you can also start looking at
properties that have a yard that's big enough for a pool.
Alternatively, the subdivision may have a community
pool that will meet your needs and give you the
opportunity to socialize with your neighbors.

### *Tip #45. Check the History*

Your real estate agent may have the ability to check
in the MLS and see when the property was first listed
for sale and whether or not there have been any price
adjustments. This is useful information to have when
you are considering an offer price. Reductions in the
list price are an indication of a motivated seller who
might be willing to accept a low offer. Sellers who
have had properties on the market for six months might
also be more willing to negotiate than someone who
listed the property six days ago.

### *Tip #46. Ask for Service Warranty*

Initial offers often include various requests by the
buyer, which the seller may or may not accept. One
common request is for the sellers to pay for a service
warranty on older appliances and air-conditioning
units. The plans differ, but most have a reasonable

annual fee and replace appliances if they can't be repaired. Don't be upset if the seller denies the request, but you might want to consider purchasing the contract for yourself. That added protection may increase your comfort level in purchasing a home with older appliances.

### Tip #47. Ask for Seller Concessions

In addition to a service warranty, a buyer can also ask the seller to contribute a percentage of the sales price toward the buyer's closing costs. Ask your loan officer what the maximum limit is for your particular loan product. If the yard is in dire need of professional landscaping or the house really needs painting, ask the seller to credit you a specific amount of money at the closing to pay for the improvements. It doesn't hurt to ask, and you may get at least part of what you requested.

### Tip #48. Remember Cash is King

Sellers are often willing to accept a lower offer if the buyer is paying cash. This is because cash sales have no financing or appraisal contingencies that could wreck the deal. The sellers have a higher level of confidence that the transaction will close with a cash offer, so they'll accept less money. Make sure that you print out your bank statement, black-out the account numbers and email it to your real estate agent because the seller will want proof that you actually have enough cash to pay what is owed at the closing. Your agent will submit the bank statement along with the written offer. Stocks and mutual fund accounts are acceptable as proof of funds, as long as they can be liquidated prior to closing.

## *Tip #49. Request Home Inspection Report*

Prospective buyers can usually cancel a purchase contract if problems are found during a home inspection. This applies to as-is contracts as well. The main difference between an as-is contract and a "normal" contract is that in the "normal" contract the seller is obligated to pay a certain amount of money toward repairing any reported problems; the seller has no such obligation in an as-is contract.

A home inspection should be conducted by a professional inspector and not your handyman. Experienced inspectors can alert the buyer to hidden issues including problems with appliances, evidence of a plumbing leak behind the walls, a hot-water tank that is near the end of its effective life, electrical problems, and inefficient heating and cooling systems. All of these items can be expensive to repair or replace.

The buyer should pick their own home inspector or ask the real estate agent for the names of three recommended companies and choose one of those. Know ahead of time what company you are hiring and make sure that you are sent the inspection report. I am saying this because some unscrupulous real estate agents may hire a "friendlier" inspector to re-do the inspection if extensive damage is discovered. In that situation, the buyer would never see the original report that states the roof needs replacing. It is unfortunate that a few bad apples can ruin things for everyone, but the potential for criminal behavior exists in every profession. Protect yourself and ask that the inspector email the report directly to you.

Keep a copy of the inspection reports in your files because it may be useful when you purchase or renew a homeowner's property insurance policy. The insurance agent will have questions about the type of construction materials in the home, and that information is in the report.

### *Tip #50. Request a Copy of Appraisal*

When you apply for a mortgage loan, the lender sends an appraiser to look at the property and estimate its value. If the appraisal value is lower than the offer price, the buyer can do one of three things: cancel the contract if it contains an appraisal contingency clause; negotiate with the seller to lower the sales price to the appraisal value; or pay the difference between the sales price and appraisal value in cash at the closing. The lender uses the appraisal value as the basis for the loan. Therefore, if the borrower chooses to pay the difference, he needs to bring a larger down payment if the appraisal value comes in low.

Federal law mandates that buyers have a right to a copy of the paid appraisal upon request. One of the most important bits of information in the report for a homeowner is the actual square footage of the home. This information will come in handy later when you want to sell the home.

### *Tip #51. Obtain Title Insurance*

Title insurance protects buyers and lenders against past defects in title that might undermine the legality of the property ownership. Defects include prior forged documents, undisclosed heirs, existing liens, and claims by ex-spouses. The insurance pays for the attorney and court costs needed to correct title problems and the payment of any liens that missed discovery during the initial lien search that preceded the issuance of the policy. Don't ever purchase a property without obtaining a title insurance policy.

The homeowner's policy is a one-time closing cost to either the buyer or seller; local custom usually determines which party pays, but this is negotiable. Federal law states that the individual paying for title insurance has the right to choose the title insurance company.

If the seller owned the property for 10 years or less, request a reissue of the seller's title policy. Title companies won't volunteer the information, but a reissue can save the buyer as much as 60 percent of the cost of a new issue. The insurance agent will want a copy of the seller's policy, so have your real estate agent request it as part of the offer. In turn, she'll send it over to your title company when she receives it.

### _Tip #52. Request a Property Survey_

Lenders require a property survey, but you should request one even if you're paying cash unless the property is a condominium or a townhouse governed by a condominium association. In this case, the surrounding land is considered a common area and is not included in the sale of the unit.

The surveyor determines if a neighbor has built anything over your property line, and most buyers appreciate a schematic drawing of the lot that shows the property boundary lines and setbacks. The drawing comes in handy if you want to install a fence, swimming pool or build an addition to the home. Most properties will have a designated setback at the property line between adjoining lots, from the street and from any body of water. A setback is an area where you are not allowed to build; you can plant hedges but no permanent structures. Any new permanent structure requires a city-issued permit, and the inspector won't approve anything that disregards the restricted areas.

Look at your survey before you start planning a project.

# 5

---

## Investor Concerns

Real estate investors buy property for a number of reasons including getting a quick profit from flipping the property, generating cash flow from rental income, holding the property for its future appreciation value and to serve as a tax shelter. Except for the flipper, these aren't necessarily mutually exclusive goals. The best of all possible worlds happens when you buy a property that generates significant cash flow, appreciates in value and provides tax sheltering for the income.

### *Tip #53. Protect Your Assets*

Talk to a good real estate attorney or insurance agent before you start to purchase investment properties. We live in a litigious society where people want to sue the individual with the deepest pockets. If your tenant's dog bites a neighbor, that neighbor might decide that you probably have more money than your tenant and come after you for medical bills as well as pain and suffering. You want to either have a large general liability policy or own property as a corporation or trust. Don't risk losing your primary residence because of something that happened at one of your income properties.

In addition to protecting yourself from lawsuits, an experienced real estate attorney can suggest ways to legally shelter property from estate taxes that will be assessed upon your death, thereby allowing you to leave more assets to your heirs. This applies to your primary residence as well as investment properties.

Play it smart and plan ahead.

### Tip #54. Join an Investment Club

Real estate investment is a popular activity, and there's a high probability that you can find an investment club near where you live or online. Hearing stories from other investors allows you to avoid their pitfalls and get valuable advice from experienced like-minded entrepreneurs. Keep an open mind until you can verify their track record because some of what you hear is apt to be false bragging that's not backed up by tangible results.

## *Tip #55. Request Association Rules and Regulations*

Although any prospective buyer should make sure
the initial offer includes the request for condo or
homeowner's association documents, it is particularly
necessary for investors to do so. Many communities
throughout the country don't allow the property to be
leased at all or not in the first or second years of new
ownership. If you find out the rules after the closing,
it's too late to do anything about it. You don't want to
find yourself sitting on a vacant property for a year or
more before you can lease it.

## *Tip #56. Take Photographs*

Take photographs before a tenant moves in so that
you have visual documentation of the unit's original
condition. Take more photographs after the tenants
move out if you are planning to make a claim for
damages and want to keep all or part of the security
deposit.

## *Tip #57. Consider Using Custom Leases*

The real estate agents in your state may only be
allowed to use leases that they can download from the
state's Realtor Association, which have been approved
by the state's supreme court. That is the case in
Florida. The Florida agents are only allowed to assist
a tenant in filling in the blanks and may not alter or

add addendums to the state-approved lease. Landlords, however, can use whatever lease they want as long as the licensees are hands-off.

The standard lease might be fine when you are first starting your investing career, but you may want an attorney to draft you a different one as you gain more experience. For example, you might want to include a condition that the landlord or his representative reserves the right to enter the property for an inspection once a month following a 24-hour notice, and that the inspector will use a key to gain access if the tenant is not home. You may also want to limit the amount of times a tenant can call for a minor repair; i.e., changing an inside light bulb, or unclogging a sink or toilet. Over time, you'll compile a list of the aggravations that annoy you the most.

Make sure that any lease you use allows the property to be shown to prospective buyers once it is listed for sale. You should include wording that a lockbox containing the house key will be placed on the front door if the tenant doesn't cooperate. Discuss this with the attorney who is drafting the lease.

### *Tip #58. Have the Tenant Pay Utilities*

Unless city ordinances prohibit it or the utilities are included in the condo's maintenance fee, have the tenants pay for the electricity, water and gas. Otherwise, you may find yourself in the position of paying a sky-high bill if they are angry at you and intentionally leave the water running or air conditioner on high while they are away. Once the lease is signed, there's not much you can do about it.

### *Tip #59. Read the Landlord and Tenant Act*

If you're planning to manage your own rental property, the first thing you need to do is to read your state's Landlord and Tenant Act. As a landlord, you can't do everything you may wish to do at one time or another. You can't walk into a unit whenever you want, or change the locks or turn off the utilities in order to force a tenant out. If you do these things, you are apt to find yourself talking to a tenant's attorney or legal aid representative. Learn the law and follow it if you want to save yourself some avoidable headaches. The rules are there to protect both parties, including you.

### *Tip #60. Hire a Property Manager*

Many investors have neither the patience nor the time to manage their own property and need to turn to professional help. Ask real estate agents or fellow investment club members for recommendations. Pricing will vary depending on your location and required services; in South Florida, investors can expect to pay between 5-10 percent of the monthly rent for property management services.

Owners who want to be completely hands-off give the property management company's real estate broker power-of-attorney to sign all leases and contracts on their behalf. These types of people don't want to know the day-to-day details about what's going on; they just want it done in an efficient manner. These property managers collect the rents, deduct their fees, pay for repairs and deposit the monthly profits in the owners' accounts.

## *Tip #61. Screen Tenants*

Pay a screening service to run a criminal background check on leasing applicants. You don't want the police kicking in the front door to bust up a brothel or a drug ring. Moreover, you sure as heck don't want someone turning your property into a meth lab or marijuana greenhouse.

You also probably want to retrieve the tenant's credit report. Experian.com allows individuals to pay for a credit report and grant other people access to see the report online for free. This is an ideal situation for landlords. Just make sure the name on the report matches the tenant's driver license. In bad economic times, many people are going to have very poor credit and need to rent for a few years until their credit score and income improve. If you are going to set a minimum allowable credit score, you need to apply it to all applicants or face the possibility of discrimination charges.

## Tip #62. Consider Government Subsidies

The U.S. Department of Housing and Urban Development (HUD) provides funds to local public housing agencies to support a Section 8 voucher program that provides subsidized housing for low-income and elderly people. The program generally pays market rents for the units. The amount of the tenant's contribution toward the monthly rental payment is based on the household's annual gross income. The housing agency pays its portion to the landlord through direct deposit, and it's the landlord's responsibility to collect the tenant's share. The housing agency doesn't screen the tenant's criminal background, so the landlord should check it out. The tenant can be evicted for non-payment while the landlord continues to receive the agency's share of the rent for the remainder of the lease.

Any clean, safe property may qualify as a potential Section 8 home including condos, townhouses, single-family homes and multi-family units. If you are looking for a tenant, register online at section8.com and list your property free of charge. Once you do that, individuals with vouchers can find your property and contact you about showing it to them. Vouchers are transferable between states so your listing is visible to everyone.

If the tenant likes it, they go to the local housing agency to complete paperwork and retrieve the lease addendums for the landlord that are added to the landlord's standard lease. A Section 8 inspector comes to the property to verify that it's clean, safe and has screens in the windows. Once that step is done, the tenant can move into the home. The landlord can collect a security deposit paid by the tenant.

Unfortunately, some Section 8 tenants don't take care of the property. If there is damage, you'll want to report it immediately to the housing authority and request repairs or compensation; if you wait until the tenant vacates the property, you may not receive anything for repairs other than your right to make a claim on the security deposit. There is a long waiting list for the voucher program, so most of the properties are kept in decent condition because the tenants don't want to run the risk of having their vouchers terminated.

# 6

---

# Distressed Property Concerns

Distressed properties usually result from owners who can no longer afford to make mortgage payments. These are the foreclosure and short sale properties that typically sell for less than market value. While this might present an attractive acquisition opportunity, both buyers and sellers need to educate themselves about the special challenges that exist when working with these types of properties.

The first thing to know is that circumstances differ depending on the state where the property is located. The United States is roughly divided in half between what are called judicial and non-judicial states. Judicial states are most common in the eastern half of the country and require lenders to file a lawsuit against the borrower and process the action through the court system in order to foreclose. This can take months or even years if the borrower retains a defense attorney, and the court calendar is clogged with pending cases.

The non-judicial states are predominately in the western half of the U.S. In these states, the borrower has a deed of trust that authorizes the lender to quickly foreclose outside of the court although the borrowers are still entitled to a court hearing if they want to file a lawsuit to defend themselves against the action.

The second thing to be aware of is that foreclosure properties actually consist of three different types. The first of these is the pre-foreclosure period when the seller has stopped making mortgage payments but still owns the home. This could mean the seller is motivated and wants to sell before a foreclosure affects his credit score; a prospective buyer will have more time to pursue these distressed homeowners in a judicial state. Secondly, if the borrower offers no foreclosure defense or all the attempts are futile, the court usually orders a public foreclosure auction of the property; check with your local courthouse to see if the auctions are held online or at a physical location if you're interested in bidding on property. Lastly, if the property fails to sell at auction, the lender takes possession and will eventually sell it; these properties are known as "real estate owned" or REOs.

A short sale occurs when a borrower's mortgage loan balance is higher than the market value of the property, and the lender agrees to accept the market value sale proceeds to pay off all (or part) of the loan and release the mortgage lien. Homeowners wishing to complete a short sale must usually provide evidence that they are suffering from some type of hardship, which makes them unable to pay the loan balance. Qualifying hardships differ among lenders and criteria may change over time. Check with an attorney who specializes in negotiating short sales for the latest information.

Each of these different types of situations requires specialized knowledge to facilitate a successful outcome. Do your homework, study the rest of this chapter and contact an experienced real estate attorney for professional advice on particular situations.

### *Tip #63. Explore Alternatives*

Because your real estate agent doesn't earn a commission unless a property is sold or leased, she may not take the time to learn about foreclosure alternatives. That's unfortunate since you may be able to find a way to stay in the home.

If you don't want to move, contact your loan servicer and ask them to explain your options including refinancing the loan at a lower interest rate or obtaining a loan modification that reduces your monthly mortgage payment. Following a housing bubble burst, there are many underwater borrowers who watch the value of their homes decline until it is less than the mortgage balance. Generally, a widespread collapse in the housing market leads to a national recession, and the government might step in to try to normalize the market. There may be programs for owner-occupied as well as investment properties, and programs for underwater borrowers who are current or late on mortgage payments. If you don't qualify for a government program, the lender may have a suitable in-house program that allows you to stay put.

However, it may not be wise to completely trust an institution whose sole purpose is to make money. If your own lender tells you that you don't qualify for a government program, get a second opinion. Unscrupulous lenders may intentionally mislead their customers in order to push them to use a less favorable in-house program that generates more money for the lender than the government programs.

Make it a point to learn what options are available to help you.

### *Tip #64. Read Your Mail*

While burying your head in the sand is an understandable impulse for a distressed homeowner, you need to open your mail from your lender or loan servicer. Ignore the late-payment statements if you wish, but pay attention to negotiation offers. If you don't open the letter, you'll never see the offer, which may be worth thousands of dollars.

One example of what you might be missing is an offer of a substantial amount of money from the lender if you'll agree to a short sale rather than a foreclosure.

This is most likely to occur in a judicial state when the lender or investor holding the note wishes to avoid a lengthy and expensive lawsuit against the homeowner. At the current time, offers of $40,000 or more are not uncommon; it all depends on the motivation of the interested parties. Some lenders may honor these offers even after the expiration date, but some may not. Read your mail.

### *Tip #65. Inspect the Property*

Distressed properties often sell well below market value, and this fact tempts some buyers to purchase these types of properties without ever seeing them. The assumption seems to be that if the price is cheap enough, there will be plenty of funds available for repairs. Unfortunately, that kind of reasoning may lead to some nasty surprises for the buyers.

If the homeowner had financial problems, routine maintenance was probably neglected, and small problems could have escalated to major ones. In addition, foreclosed homes are often empty for months before they sell, and vagrants as well as the elements have had the opportunity to inflict a considerable amount of damage.

Roofs can be very expensive to replace, and broken windows lead to moldy interiors, which are a hassle to clean. Electrical and plumbing problems can be costly to fix, and appliances are often stolen from vacant homes. In addition, what do you do if you find a sinkhole in the backyard that is threatening the stability of the home? Too bad; all sales are final. There are no seller disclosures prior to a foreclosure auction or REO sale. You should have looked.

Hire an inspector to search for problems if you aren't qualified to assess the damage. Even properties that are scheduled for auction are often available for viewing during an open house before the auction date. Presumably, you're buying the property because it was priced attractively. Things won't look so pretty if the cost of the repairs exceeds the savings you realized on the sale price. If you throw in the joy of working with contractors, you might find the purchase to be more of a headache and less of a deal. Live and learn.

### *Tip #66. Conduct a Lien Search*

A lien is the recorded evidence of a debt, and a foreclosure is the enforcement of the lien. Generally, lien priority is determined by the date and time of recording, and  the priority dictates in what order creditors are paid from the proceeds of a sale. However, state law can designate super liens that have a higher priority than mortgage liens regardless of when the super lien was recorded. Property taxes, special assessments, government liens, code violations, and utility liens are some common high-priority liens. So, why do you care?

You care if you buy a property at a foreclosure auction. The lien priority determines the order in which lienholders are paid from the proceeds of a sale. A foreclosure auction usually wipes out all the junior liens (such as credit card companies and homeowner associations), which have a lower priority than the party bringing the foreclosure lawsuit, but the successful bidder may be on the hook for paying the superior liens if the auction failed to generate enough money to satisfy their claims.

For example, city code-violation fees may be assessed daily on an abandoned property, and these liens can survive a foreclosure. So, suppose a property has an unpaid loan balance of $140,000 and a market value of $200,000. The foreclosing lender sets the minimum bid at $140,000. You're the only bidder and walk away thinking that you got a great deal. However, after the sale, you discover that there is a $100,000 code-violation penalty that now belongs to you. Instead of flipping the property for a nice profit, you have to pay the city what's due plus daily fees until the violations are corrected. Good job! Next time you'll do your homework. Do yourself a favor and pay a title company $100 to conduct a lien search on prospective properties.

### Tip #67. Verify Foreclosing Entity on Auction Property

Be sure to check which lienholder is responsible for the foreclosure auction because only the liens that are junior to the initiating party are wiped out. The successful bidder is responsible for the senior liens if the sale proceeds are insufficient to pay them off. Many homeowners obtain multiple mortgages, and the order of priority is determined by the date and time of recording.

Suppose the property was purchased in 2008 with a $150,000 loan. Property values appreciated, and the homeowners took out a $75,000 second mortgage in 2010. In 2013, neighborhood property values fell, and the homeowners stopped making the payments on the second mortgage. The subordinate (second) lender initiated the foreclosure action. You see a $175,000 home listed for auction with a minimum bid of $75,000, and you jump on it. Too late, you realize that the junior mortgage holder initiated the foreclosure, and you now owe the first mortgage lender $150,000.

The same type of scenario happens when a homeowner's association (HOA) forecloses in states where association liens aren't considered super liens. In these states, the HOA lien is always junior to the mortgage liens because the lender would not have approved a new mortgage if the homeowner wasn't paying the association fees. Consequently, HOA liens are recorded at a later date and have lower priority. If you participate in an HOA foreclosure auction, and the proceeds of the sale aren't sufficient to pay off the mortgage balance, any mortgages on the property become your responsibility. Some investors intentionally buy these properties at auction with the idea that they can rent them out, recoup their investment and make a profit before the lender forecloses.

Remember that it's only the junior liens that are "automatically" cleared by a foreclosure auction. The purchaser is buying "subject to" the liens.

### Tip #68. Slow Down When IRS Tax Lien Is on Auction Property

IRS tax liens will always be junior to mortgage liens because a lender would never approve a loan with an existing tax lien. The successful auction bidder is not responsible for paying the lien, but he might lose the property. This is because the IRS has a 120-day redemption period in which to purchase the property from the bidder. The purchase price includes interest, prorated property tax and insurance, legal fees and reimbursement for any payments made to senior lienholders. Any improvements that the winning bidder made to the property are not reimbursed. Therefore, you may want to wait to remodel until 120 days after the auction if the property is encumbered by an IRS tax lien.

### Tip #69. Know Your State's Right of Redemption Laws

Foreclosed homeowners may also have a state-legislated right of redemption to buy back a property after a foreclosure auction. This right of redemption may prevent title from transferring and give the homeowner the right to stay in the property without making mortgage payments until the end of the redemption period even if there are no plans to redeem the property. In other states, ownership transfers to the auction buyer, but the previous owner retains the right to reclaim it during the redemption period, which can be anywhere from a few days to 18 months. State law dictates the formula for calculating the repurchase price. It might be a reimbursement of the purchase cost, or it could be the payment of the entire loan balance if the winning bidder was the lender. Check with a local real estate attorney for more information.

### Tip #70. Track Auction Buyers

Another source for discounted properties is the auction buyer who may be happy to flip the property to you for a profit. If it can sell without the services of a real estate agent, the flipper saves the cost of the real estate commission and keeps more money in his pocket. Auction sales are recorded in searchable public records that include the buyer's name and address. Identify pre-foreclosure property you're interested in, and if you fail to submit the winning bid, contact the buyer after the sale is recorded. Verify if liens are present and adjust the offer price accordingly. You may be able to purchase the property well below market value. Remember to inspect it first if possible.

### Tip #71. Heed the Advice of Your Real Estate Agent

Real estate agents aren't usually involved in county foreclosure auctions, but they do play a critical role in REO transactions. Pick someone with experience in this type of property and then follow his advice.

The forces of supply and demand influence the prices of the REO bank-owned foreclosures. When the marketplace is flooded with REO inventory, the prices go down; likewise, prices rise when the REO listings are scarcer. If your agent recommends that you offer $100,000, don't waste everybody's time and insist on offering $50,000 just because it's an REO. Unless you have studied the local marketplace, listen to the expert.

### Tip #72. Submit a Compelling Foreclosure Offer

Everybody wants to save money, and foreclosures garner a lot of attention from prospective buyers. It's not unusual for the listing agent to receive 20 or more offers the first week the property is listed in the MLS. Therefore, you want your offer to be as strong as possible, and there are a few things you can do to give yourself an edge over the competition.

Typical sales contracts have a number of contingencies that allow a buyer to cancel the contract and recover the good faith money. These contingencies are the home inspection, appraisal and loan approval. Consequently, if you submit an offer in which you waive these contingencies, you have a better chance of having your offer accepted by the lender.

The first thing you can do to improve your position is to have a property inspection before you submit the offer. Then, submit an offer with zero days for the inspection period and no money for repairs. This one step makes your offer more attractive than many of the submissions.

The next thing you can do if you have the funds, is to offer cash for the property rather than obtaining a loan. This eliminates the need for an appraisal, and loan approval is no longer an issue. This will put you at the top of the pack, and the lack of contingencies is the reason why many lenders will accept a lower cash offer before they accept a higher financed offer.

Finally, you need to realize that lenders are under no obligation to negotiate the terms of the offer with you, and they usually want to close quickly. That's why your first offer should be your highest and best offer, and if you're paying cash, offer to close in less than 30 days.

### Tip #73. Consider an FHA Foreclosure Home

The Federal Housing Administration (FHA) is an agency within the U.S. Department of Housing and Urban Development (HUD). FHA mortgage loans are popular with consumers because of their lenient underwriting guidelines and low down payment requirements, and they are popular with lenders because the FHA insures the lenders from suffering any loss on the loans. If there is a foreclosure and the property sells for less than the loan balance, the FHA will pay the difference to the lender. Because of this, HUD controls the way in which FHA foreclosure homes are sold.

These HUD homes appear in the MLS listings as REO properties, and prospective buyers can view and inspect them prior to making an offer. However, only a HUD-approved real estate professional can submit the offer, and all offers are submitted online at Hudhomestore.com. Interested buyers can also search for FHA foreclosures and HUD-approved real estate brokers on this website.

### *Tip #74. Search HomePath and HomeSteps Websites*

Fannie Mae and Freddie Mac are two government-sponsored enterprises that purchase a large number of mortgage loans from lenders. When these homes become foreclosures, the properties are listed in the MLS with showing instructions. Real estate licensees, on behalf of their buyers, submit purchase offers online at homepath.com (Fannie Mae) or homesteps.com (Freddie Mac). Properties that fail to sell online are offered at auctions around the country.

At the present time (2013), both entities offer favorable financing terms for qualified borrowers using one of their approved lenders. Low down payment, no appraisal and bulk sales to qualified investors are three of the most attractive features. HomePath currently has a renovation mortgage available in which the borrower can include costs for improvements in the mortgage. Check the websites for the most current options.

### *Tip #75. Learn the Facts About Short Sales*

The possibility for a short sale occurs when the seller's mortgage balance is greater than the current market value of the home (this is called being upside-down or underwater), and the seller asks the lender to "forgive" the difference between the two amounts. In other words, the lender accepts the shortfall and releases the mortgage lien on the property, which allows the buyer to have clear title to the property. The buyer is not allowed to be a relative of the seller; it must be an arm's-length transaction, or both buyer and seller may be found guilty of fraud.

Lenders don't necessarily approve short sales for all underwater sellers. Many lenders want proof of a financial hardship before they approve the transaction. Once approved, the lender agrees to pay the real estate commission and other closing costs generally paid for by the seller. The seller may even be eligible to receive incentive money for selling (more about this in tip #81.)

## *Tip #76. Have a Professional Negotiate the Short Sale*

Negotiating with a lender is a time-consuming process, and if there is more than one mortgage on the property (such as an equity line of credit), the approval process becomes even more laborious. Multiple phone calls, tracking documents and getting all the parties to agree on the terms is work that's best left to the professionals, which could be the seller's real estate agent, a title company that specializes in short sales or a real estate attorney.

## *Tip #77. Request a Release from Liability for Deficiency*

When a borrower obtains a mortgage loan, he must sign two documents: the mortgage and the note. In the mortgage, the borrower pledges the property as collateral for the loan and grants the lender the right to reclaim the property if the borrower does not comply with the terms of the agreement. A foreclosure is the enforcement of the mortgage lien on the property. On the other hand, the note is the borrower's IOU. In some states, the lenders may also file a lawsuit if the note is not fully paid off. Therefore, sellers involved in short sale transactions must make sure that they have a signed document from the lender that states the lender will not make a claim on any portion of the remaining balance on the mortgage note. Only an attorney can give a legal opinion as to the legal sufficiency of the lender's letter. Don't assume that the lender is acting on your behalf. That isn't the case, and many lenders may not voluntarily submit a release from liability letter; you or your negotiator may have to request it.

### *Tip #78. Write Your Own Short Sale Hardship Letter*

The seller should write his own hardship letter that explains why he cannot repay the lender the entire amount that's owed. Some possible reasons include illness, death or disability of the homeowner or family member; loss of job or reduction in wages; forced job relocation; divorce or separation; incarceration; pending bankruptcy; rapidly adjusting mortgage interest rates; little or no money down when the house was initially purchased; inability to pay mortgage, property tax, credit card or homeowner's insurance; and insufficient resources to make needed repairs. Some lenders may accept a declining real estate market as a sufficient reason. The negotiator should be able to advise you on the specific requirements, but you must write the letter yourself.

### *Tip #79. Submit Required Short Sale Documentation*

The exact amount of required paperwork depends on the individual lender; however, Fannie Mae has a financial worksheet that many of the lenders will want you to submit as part of your short sale package. You can view Form 710 at https://www.fanniemae.com/content/guide_form/710.pdf.

One of the primary reasons for a lender not approving a short sale is the lack of documentation. Submit everything the lender requests including bank statements, tax returns, hardship letter, divorce decree, separation agreement, medical bills, death certificate, and proof of all earned income.

### *Tip #80. Obtain a Preemptive Short Sale Lien Search*

Many homeowners attempting a short sale have already stopped making mortgage payments and are trying to complete the transaction before the lender foreclosures. Consequently, they want to process to be as smooth as possible without any unexpected delays. Therefore, it's recommended that a title company perform a lien search before the property is under contract. That allows the title company to clear up any issues before a buyer or lender is involved in the transaction. Short sales can take a considerable amount of time to complete, and you want to avoid any unnecessary stresses on a buyer; having to discuss obstacles with a lender just adds to the timeframe. Get the problems resolved early in the process. Be aware that the title company may charge a minimal fee for this service.

### *Tip #81. Investigate Lender's Monetary Short Sale Incentives*

Most lenders don't keep residential mortgage loans in their own portfolio; the loans are sold to Fannie Mae, Freddie Mac, other lenders, life insurance companies and other investors. In return, the lenders receive funds that they can use to make more loans, and the purchasers receive the income stream that's generated by the monthly mortgage payments. Everything works as planned until the homeowners stop making their mortgage payments, and the investors are left with non-performing loans on their books. At that point, the investors may be willing to incentivize the homeowners to sell their property. How much, if anything, they are willing to pay depends on the motivation of the entity or individual who owns the note. In 2013, some individuals were receiving $40,000 or more when they completed a short sale of their home. Your negotiator can research this opportunity for you.

Be sure to open letters from your lender because they may contain an offer that includes a deadline in which to act. Some investors will pay even after the deadline passes, and some won't. The letters should be on file with the lender, and you shouldn't have to produce the original. But, anything can happen. Open your mail and keep the offer letters.

### _Tip #82. Short Sale Buyers Need to Be Patient_

A typical short sale involving one lender is likely to close in 120 days or less. If there are multiple lenders, it may take significantly longer. So be prepared. Have your real estate agent stay in touch with the lender or seller's negotiator and make sure she keeps you informed. Have her ask the listing agent for detailed information on the negotiator. If the seller is doing his own negotiating or the listing agent sounds confused about the process, you probably want to move on to another property. Chances are fairly high that this deal will never close.

# 7

---

## Financing Concerns

Financing is the lifeblood of a robust real estate market. While there will always be cash buyers, borrowed money allows prospective purchasers to obtain a more valuable property than what many could afford if they had to pay in cash. Investors, in particular, appreciate the value of financing. By using positive leverage and borrowed money, they can buy multiple properties instead of one; rent them out with positive cash flow and hold them a few years as the value appreciates. When the time is right, the smart investor can sell them, invest the proceeds in additional property and postpone the payment of any capital gains tax. They can accomplish this and build their wealth by using very little of their own money. However, both buyers and sellers first need to know the financing basics in order to maximize their profits.

## *Tip #83. Understand the Basic Types of Loans*

If you don't have much cash, but your credit is good, then you are a prime candidate for a mortgage loan. The two main categories of residential financing are ones that involve government assurances to reimburse lenders for losses (FHA, VA and USDA), and conventional loans that have no government intervention for losses.

The first thing you need to know is that the government loans aren't available for investment properties unless you are planning to live in one of the units of a duplex, triplex or fourplex. If that's the case, make sure your loan officer is aware of that fact. Government loans are attractive because they require low (or no) down payment and may allow the borrower to have a higher debt-to-income ratio than a conventional loan.

Federal Housing Administration (FHA) loans are available throughout the country, but there are maximum loan limits that are determined for each individual county within a state. In 2013, the required down payment was 3.5 percent of the purchase price. Lenders are 100 percent insured against losses by the U.S. government.

The U.S. Department of Veteran Affairs (VA) guarantees the VA loans that provide veterans, active military service members and surviving spouses with the means to obtain affordable housing. The VA reimburses the lender a certain portion of any losses suffered as a result of a foreclosure or short sale. In 2013, 100 percent financing with no money down was available to qualified applicants.

The U.S. Department of Agriculture (USDA) guarantees the USDA loans that are intended for lower income, rural borrowers. In 2013, 100 percent financing with no money down was available to qualified applicants.

Government loans are assumable by qualified borrowers; a non-vet can even assume a VA loan. Why is this important? It's important if the seller's interest rate on a government loan is lower than the current rate being offered on similar mortgages. The qualified borrower can receive a new note with the same interest rate and payment schedule as the seller's loan. This can save someone thousands of dollars in interest payments and help them qualify for a more expensive home. Therefore, if you are the seller and have such a loan, make sure that you tell your listing agent, so she can highlight the attractive assumable interest rate in the MLS listing and in her advertising. It might help you sell the home faster and for a higher price.

Your next option is a conventional loan that in 2013 required a minimum 5 percent down payment in most of the country. In states that were hit hard by foreclosures, the minimum down payment might be 20 percent. Unlike the government loans, these loans are also available for residential non-owner-occupied investment properties. If you obtain an investment loan, don't be surprised if the interest rate is higher than what you see displayed in ads or on the Internet. Investment loans are riskier for the lender, so the interest rate may be as much as one percent more than the rate for an owner-occupied property. The loans are riskier because an investor who is having financial problems is more likely to stop making mortgage payments on an investment property before he stops making payments for his principal residence.

### *Tip #84. Explore Unconventional Alternatives*

If you have some cash, but won't qualify for a conventional mortgage loan, you might want to contact a hard-money lender. These lenders don't care about your credit score, but they will charge you an interest rate that is significantly higher than the going-rate. They may also require that you contribute 25 percent or more of the sale price as a down payment and closing costs can be quite high.

On the other hand, if you have some cash available for a down payment and the seller has already paid off his mortgage, you might want to ask if the seller would consider financing your mortgage loan. You receive a loan at interest rates that are probably lower than those offered by a hard-money lender, and the seller receives a steady stream of income at an interest rate that is higher than his savings account. Your real estate attorney can draft the documents, and everyone signs as usual at the closing.

Maybe you're reading this and wondering if you can become an investor with little cash and bad credit. The answer is yes; you just need to find a partner who's willing to invest with you. In return for a share of the profits, you will find suitable properties and maybe contribute some cash or offer to manage the properties for him. Have an attorney draw up the contract or review a potential partner's agreement before you sign anything. You may be able to find interested buyers by searching the tax records for individuals or corporations that own multiple properties in a particular city or county. If they already own some, chances are good that at least one of them will want to own more. One interested person is all it takes to get you started.

### *Tip #85. Consider a Short-Term Loan*

Individuals (flippers) who are looking to renovate properties and quickly re-sell them may want to consider a short-term adjustable-rate mortgage. In general, a shorter term means a lower starting interest rate. Know your real estate market before you make this type of commitment because you want to avoid the situation where the rate starts to increase before you sell the property.

## *Tip #86. Amortize the Costs of Repairs*

Individuals who want to purchase fixer-uppers often pay cash because it's difficult to have a normal mortgage loan approved when the property is damaged. However, there are currently (2013) FHA and Fannie Mae products that target these types of buyers.

The first program is the FHA 203(k) Renovation Loan for owner-occupied properties of 1-4 units. The borrower receives funds based on an as-approved appraisal value. Besides being used for basic repairs such as roofing, plumbing and electrical, the funds may be approved for enhancements such as room additions and decks. The lender deposits the improvement funds in an escrow account and oversees the progress of the work. Because of the required oversight, not all FHA lenders offer 203(k) loans. Check with the major banks first. If they don't offer this product, they may point you to a lender who does.

The FHA also offers a loan program for commercial investors. The FHA Section 221(d)(4) product is a multi-family new construction and rehabilitation loan for apartment buildings with five or more units. The fact that this is a combined construction loan/ permanent financing product with low interest rates and a 40-year amortization term make this an attractive loan for many investors.

Fannie Mae foreclosure homes that need moderate repair or modernization may be eligible for the HomePath Renovation Mortgage. The program is available to both owner-occupants and investors who are interested in financing the purchase of a 1-4 unit structure. The funded loan may include a maximum of $35,000 additional money to apply toward improvements. Interested borrowers can find eligible properties and approved lenders at http://homepath. com.

### *Tip #87. Take Advantage of Assistance Programs*

HUD distributes funds that state agencies use for a variety of purposes including down payment assistance for eligible applicants. Go to http://portal.hud.gov/ hudportal/HUD?src=/states for more information.

### *Tip #88. Use Retirement Funds*

Three of the most popular retirement plans (in 2013) are the IRA, Roth IRA and the 401(k). While this section is not intended to make anyone an investment expert, it's good to know the basic advantages and disadvantages of the different plans and how they can be used to purchase real estate. Please contact a financial planner or CPA for current IRS laws regarding these types of accounts.

A traditional IRA allows any income-earning individual to contribute to an account until the age of 70 1/2. Penalty-free qualified distributions can begin at age 59 1/2 and must start by age 70 1/2. Early withdrawals are subject to a 10 percent penalty fee. Traditional IRAs allow the investor to claim a tax deduction the year the contributions were made and future withdrawals are taxed as ordinary income. This may be a good choice if you anticipate your tax bracket to be lower when you retire.

The Roth IRA is significantly different from a traditional IRA. It has maximum income limitations for contributors; contributions can continue after age 70 1/2; there is no mandatory distribution requirement for the contributor although heirs must start taking distributions; contributions are not declared as tax deductions; and the withdrawals are tax-free. In addition, *contributions* can be withdrawn without penalty at any time, but you have to wait until age 59 1/2 to withdraw the *earnings* without a penalty. Furthermore, the account must be opened for five years before earnings can be withdrawn without paying taxes. This may be a good choice if you anticipate your tax bracket to be higher when you retire.

A 401(k) plan has much more generous annual contribution limits than the IRA plans, and employers can contribute a limited amount of matching funds for as long as the investor remains with the company. Deposits to a traditional 401(k) account appear on your paycheck as a pre-tax deposit; therefore, taxes are paid when the money is withdrawn. Your company may also offer a Roth 401(k) in which the contributions are deposited from after-tax income, and the withdrawals are tax-free. Companies may require that employees work for a certain number of years before the matching funds are 100 percent available for withdrawal. Self-employed individuals can establish their own solo 401(k). In general, money withdrawn prior to the investor reaching 59 1/2 years of age is subject to a 10 percent penalty fee. However, there may be hardship exceptions to this. One great feature of the 401(k) plans is that they may allow an investor to withdraw half the money in the account, to a maximum of $50,000, and pay back the loan including interest to themselves. Individual plans will stipulate the timeframe for payback.

So what does all of this information have to do with real estate? For starters, traditional IRAs allow a first-time homebuyer to engage in a penalty-free (but not tax-free) early withdrawal of $10,000 for a down payment on a new owner-occupied home. This does not have to be the first home the individual ever owned. The IRS defines a first-time homebuyer as someone who as not owned a principal residence during the past three years preceding a purchase. Roth IRAs allow *contributions* to be withdrawn anytime without a penalty, so this money can be used as a down payment. In addition, after a Roth IRA account has been open for five years, the first-time homebuyer can withdraw $10,000 of *earnings* to pay expenses without incurring the 10 percent penalty. The 401(k) investors can take out a loan for the down payment and pay themselves back with interest.

If you like what you've read so far, keep reading because things get even better if you want to use your retirement funds to buy *investment* real estate. In order to do this, you need what is called a self-directed IRA or 401(k) that allows you to choose real estate as an investment vehicle; the typical brokerage accounts only allow you to choose from stocks, bonds and mutual funds. In addition, you want this to be a self-managed account where you control the checkbook and write the checks for repairs and expenses; the alternative is to open a custodial account where an intermediary approves each expenditure and charges a processing fee for every transaction.

The rules that regulate self-directed accounts are complicated, so be sure to check with a CPA or attorney before you start using the funds to purchase real estate. Basically, the purchased property can never be occupied by the account owner; it must be acquired only for investment purposes. All the expenses related to maintaining the property must be paid for with funds from the retirement account. Likewise, all the generated rental income must be deposited in the same retirement account. Mortgage interest, property tax and depreciation are not deductible for properties in the account, and the properties cannot be sold and replaced through a 1031 exchange. Consequently, you need to think long and hard before opening an account. To maximize your profits and retain the ability to manage the property and deduct expenses, create a limited liability company (LLC) that is owned by an IRA or is a self-employed business for a solo 401(k) account. It may be difficult to obtain a mortgage using this type of business structure, so plan on paying in cash if the account has sufficient funds. However, whether you finance the deal or pay cash, the business purchases the property and can maintain it without the need to pay a professional property manager. The business can then deduct the costs for management and performing property repairs.

Because you lose the ability to participate in a 1031 exchange, you'll want to check to see if you qualify for a self-directed Roth IRA or Roth 401(k). If so, the qualified withdrawals aren't taxed as ordinary income or as capital gains. All profits are tax-free.

Check with an unbiased financial advisor for the latest rules; banks and brokerage offices may try to steer you away from this type of investment if they don't offer self-directed and self-managed accounts. Find someone who's not affiliated with a lending institution if you want to know all your options.

### *Tip #89. Restructure Your Portfolio*

Lenders may have a limit on the number of mortgaged properties you can have in your portfolio at any one time; lenders won't lend you any more money when you reach this limit. It could be as few as four properties or as many as ten; it's up to the lender. However, don't despair when you reach this wall. Talk to a commercial lender about refinancing into a collateralized mortgage loan that includes a group of your existing properties. This group will then be counted as one mortgage loan and your residential lenders will start originating loans for you once again. Repeat the process as needed.

### *Tip #90.  Learn About Small Business Administration (SBA) Loans*

Prospective business owner-occupants may want to investigate the possibility of an SBA 7(a) or 504 loan prior to sitting down with a lender. It is sometimes easier to read the background material first before a loan officer starts to discuss multiple alternatives, and you walk away feeling overwhelmed by the different loan products. This type of loan offers attractive terms and combines construction and purchase loans into one package. Contact a commercial lender if you're looking to buy office space where your business will occupy the majority of the leasable space.

# 8

---

# Tax and Regulatory Concerns

Whether you're planning to purchase one home or build a portfolio of income-producing properties, you want to maximize your profits while operating within the law. In order to do this effectively, you need to understand the tax laws as they apply to real estate and have a good working knowledge of federal housing and disclosure laws. If you are buying or constructing commercial real estate, you must be familiar with the Americans with Disabilities Act.

Contact your CPA or real estate attorney before you acquire property to make sure you have a clear understanding of the most advantageous way to hold title. A detailed discussion of asset protection is beyond the scope of this book, and you should speak to your advisor about the pros and cons of owning property as a natural person, corporation or trust.

## *Tip #91. Realize That Forgiven Mortgage Debt May Be Taxed*

The federal government requires lenders to send borrowers and the IRS a copy of Form 1099-C, Cancellation of Debt when a property sells for less than the loan balance, which is a situation that occurs in a foreclosure or a short sale. The form shows the lender's estimate of the property value and the amount of the forgiven debt that may be considered as taxable income for the year of the sale.

If the property is your primary residence, the Mortgage Forgiveness and Debt Relief Act may exempt the forgiven debt from being considered as taxable income. At the present time, this law is scheduled to terminate on December 31, 2013. The law does not apply to second homes or investment property. However, additional other exemptions may apply including bankruptcy or insolvency. The IRS defines insolvency as "You are insolvent when your total debts are more than the fair market value of your total assets."

If this topic applies to you, contact a CPA for more information.

## Tip #92. *Hold for Capital Gains Tax Rate*

The IRS considers investment real estate as a capital asset in which the profits from the sale are taxed at a lower rate than ordinary income if it is held for more than a year before it's sold. Contact your accountant for current tax rates.

If you have an investment property that you want to sell after 10 months of ownership and don't need an immediate payoff, you might want to go ahead and list it for sale but insist on a long closing date. That way, if you own it for at least one year and a day, you'll qualify for the lower tax rate on the profits.

## Tip #93. *Benefit From Capital Gains Exclusion*

If you are single or married and filing singly and have owned and lived in your primary home for two of the past five years, the first $250,000 in capital gain (profit) is exempt from taxes. You don't have to declare the profit as income; take the check at closing and spend it any way you like without worrying about what you might owe Uncle Sam. Married couples filing jointly can enjoy a $500,000 tax-free windfall. Homeowners can do this every two years. So if you don't mind moving, buy a handyman-special home that needs repairs, fix it up and sell it for a nice tax-free profit in a couple of years.

## *Tip #94. Understand Capital Loss*

Don't despair if you suffer a loss when you sell an investment property; that loss can offset your capital gains for that year. In addition, you can deduct a maximum of $3,000 in net losses in a given year, carry over any excess and apply it to the next year's tax returns.

For example, assume that in 2013 you sold two investment properties that you had owned for more than one year (thereby qualifying them as capital assets.) Furthermore, assume that you sold one for a $5,000 capital gain and the other for an $11,500 capital loss. The loss can offset the gain ($11,500 minus $5,000) leaving you with a net loss of $6,500. You can then deduct $3,000 of this net loss from your 2013 taxable income and carry over the remaining $3,500 to the next year when it will be treated as an additional capital loss. In 2014, $3,000 of the carry over can be deducted from taxable income (if there are no capital gains to offset), and the remaining $500 loss can be carried over to 2015 and treated as an additional capital loss.

Remember that it is only losses on the sale of investment property that can offset capital gains, be deducted from taxable income, and carried over to the following year. Your primary residence is not considered an investment property, and a loss on the sale of your home can't be used to offset a gain from the sale of investment property and can't be carried over to the next year.

### Tip #95. Appreciate the Value of Depreciation

Uncle Sam rewards real estate investors, and the IRS gives them a nice, big present all wrapped up in a bow. This generous gift is called depreciation and has nothing to do with the physical condition of a property. It is simply an additional tax deduction that allows investors to shelter part of the income. Depreciation is calculated using the straight-line method in which an equal amount of depreciation is depreciated for the life of the property. An owner can take the deduction on residential *investment* structures for 27.5 years and 39 years for commercial property. Land does not depreciate.

The calculation is easier than it may first appear to be. The first step is to calculate the depreciable basis for the property using the following formula: acquisition costs minus the value of the land (on tax record). The next step is to divide this result by 29.5 for residential property and by 39 for commercial property. The result is the annual amount of depreciation that you can deduct from your taxable income for the life of the asset (29.5 years or 39 years).

While it is obvious that you can no longer claim the deduction once the property is sold, you may have to pay a depreciation recapture tax the year the property sells. The government is willing to give you a tax break as long as you own property, but then wants part of it back when you sell the asset. Remember to contact your CPA for the latest tax rules and regulations.

To learn how to defer the payment of this recapture tax as well as any capital gains tax, read on! The next topic discussed is one more remarkable gift from the government to aid knowledgeable investors.

### *Tip #96. Take Advantage of a 1031 Like-Kind Exchange*

Hopefully, your tax advisor will tell you about a 1031 exchange. But, if not, be prepared to be knocked off your feet by this glorious IRS tax provision that allows an investor to indefinitely defer paying the depreciation recapture tax and the capital gains tax on profits generated by the sale of investment property.

Internal Revenue Code section 1031 provides investors with a means to exchange like-kind investment properties and defer payment of any capital gains tax. Like-kind real estate properties include everything but principal residences and second homes. You can exchange vacant lots for apartment buildings, single-family homes for vacant lots, office buildings for houses, or warehouses for duplexes. There are endless numbers of possible combinations. However, you cannot exchange real estate for artwork; they are not like-kind investments. In order for all the capital gains to be deferred, the replacement property must be at least as valuable as the relinquished property. If the replacement property is more valuable, you can "trade up" and contribute additional funds.

Any 1031 exchange includes at least two properties: a relinquished property and a replacement property. Strict rules need to be followed including one that states a qualified intermediary holds the proceeds of the sale, and that the investor never touches the funds.

In a delayed exchange, the investor has 45 days after closing on the relinquished property to notify the qualified intermediary, in writing, of possible replacement properties. Once this step is completed, the investor must close on one of the previously identified properties within 180 days of closing on the relinquished property. If all the properties identified in your list turn out to be unavailable or unsuitable, you're out of luck. Be prepared to pay the IRS the capital gains tax.

Start looking for possible replacements before the sale of the relinquished property because the number of potential replacement properties identified on the list is limited by the following three rules:

- 3-Property Rule allows a maximum of three potential properties, no matter what their value. This is the most popular choice.

- 200 Percent Rule allows any number of replacement properties as long as their total value does not exceed twice the value of the relinquished properties.

- 95 percent rule also allows any number of potential replacements, but you must close on 95 percent of the aggregate value of the identified replacement properties. This option is seldom used.

In addition to this popular delayed exchange, there are a few other variations allowed for exchanges. An Internet search quickly displays links to very informative websites. Talk to a knowledgeable tax advisor and plan ahead. Find the type of exchange that works best for your situation and start increasing the return on your investments!

### *Tip #97. Comply With Tax Law for Foreign Sellers*

The Foreign Investment in Real Property Tax Act (FIRPTA) holds the buyer responsible for ensuring that 10 percent (or another amount) of the proceeds arising from the sale of a foreign national's real estate. The withheld funds are sent by the withholding agent (usually the title company, an attorney or the buyer) to the IRS using IRS Forms 8288 and 8288-A. If the foreigner's taxes are less than the 10 percent, the IRS refunds the excess amount after the foreign seller files a tax return.

There are exceptions to FIRPTA's 10 percent rule, and the seller should contact an accountant who is familiar with U.S. tax laws. Requests to withhold a lesser amount must be submitted to the IRS using Form 8288-B. If approved, the IRS issues a Withholding Certificate, and a copy should be given to all parties involved in the closing. The seller needs to submit the request early so that the IRS has time to process the paperwork before the scheduled closing date.

### *Tip #98. Familiarize Yourself With the Fair Housing Act*

The Civil Rights Act of 1866 prevents racial discrimination in any real estate transaction (including commercial), but the Fair Housing Act was adopted in 1968 to extend protection to additional classes of people participating in *residential* real estate transactions. This Act provides a legal recourse for individuals who feel that they are victims of housing discrimination based on race, color, national origin, religion, sex, familial status and handicaps. The law was later amended to permit designated senior housing to forgo the need for special services or facilities that are specially designed for residents who are 55 or older.

The Fair Housing Act requires that covered multi-family housing with four or more units that was first occupied after March 13, 1991 have certain design features including accessible building entrances and common areas, accessible routes through the housing unit, usable doors, reachable light switches, thermostats and electrical outlets, reinforced walls so that grab bars can be installed, and usable kitchens and bathrooms.

The Fair Housing law is not all encompassing. However, it applies to many single-family housing situations including buildings owned by the federal government, any residential sales or rentals involving a real estate licensee, and any residential property owned by an active investor (someone who owns four or more residential properties, or who has sold two or more non-owner-occupied housing properties in the past two years.) The law also covers commercial multi-family housing of five or more units and non-owner-occupied multi-family homes with two-to-four units.

If we flip this law around, it becomes evident that individuals who are not working with a real estate licensee, who own a single-family property or owner-occupied properties of two-to-four units, and who are not considered active investors (as previously defined) may discriminate against a member of any of the protected classes except race.

For example, suppose someone owns a duplex and lives in one of the two units. If she doesn't want to lease the other unit to a man, she doesn't have to as long as a real estate licensee is not involved in the transaction, and she's not an active investor. In another example, perhaps a for-sale-by-owner individual doesn't want to sell to a Canadian; he doesn't have to as long as he is not considered an active investor, and the transaction didn't involve a licensee.

Unfortunately, real estate licensees continually violate the law in their advertising. It's a Fair Housing violation for the MLS listing or other marketing material to include phrases such as: walking distance to <anywhere> (violation based on handicap status), across the street from a specific place of worship (violation based on religion), and family-friendly neighborhood (violation based on familial status). Investigators do search the Internet for this type of advertising, and they do take legal action against licensees.

Real estate agents also need to be careful when showing property; they aren't allowed to steer people in or out of particular types of neighborhoods. While it may be obvious that people shouldn't be excluded from neighborhoods, the reverse situation is not as clearly understood. For example, if a buyer tells a licensee that he only wants to see properties in Hispanic areas, the real estate agent can't comply with this request. The agent should ask the prospective buyer to narrow the search criteria to a particular part of town, near a friend, or close to a specific school or church. Alternatively, the agent might suggest that the prospect drive around desirable areas and watch people as they are coming home from work; however, the agent should not accompany them on this hunt for ethnicity. The buyers may also search the Internet for ethnic grocery stores and ask to see listings in relevant areas.

Many residential properties are leased without the landlord ever meeting prospective tenants. Under no circumstances, should a licensee respond to questions regarding the race or ethnicity of the applicant. If a landlord asks, the licensee simply informs him that the licensee can't answer this type of question without violating the Fair Housing law. If the landlord insists, the licensee should withdraw from the transaction.

Everyone should be aware that individual communities or counties might have additional rules that apply. In particular, sexual orientation is being established as a protected class in many areas since federal law does not cover it.

If you are a member of a Fair Housing protected class and feel that you are the victim of discrimination, you should call the number under the "Contact Us" tab at hud.gov. Local news stations may also welcome the opportunity to air your story.

### *Tip #99. Adhere to the Americans With Disabilities Act*

The Americans with Disabilities Act (ADA) is a comprehensive law enacted to prevent discrimination against individuals with physical or mental disabilities. Title III of the Act deals with measures that owners of real estate that are open to the public must take to ensure that the rights of the disabled are protected.

While most of the law deals with commercial real estate like office buildings and retail shops, it also applies to business owners who meet with customers in their own home. Those home offices should have an accessible building entrance and a bathroom that can accommodate an individual in a wheelchair. If not, the business owner runs the risk of being on the wrong end of a lawsuit.

Contact a real estate attorney if you have questions about the suitability of your space and potential liability.

### *Tip #100. Know Your Closing Options*

There is no law that requires buyers and sellers to meet in a conference room to sign the closing documents. In fact, the buyers and sellers don't have to meet at all.

Mail-away closings are a very attractive option for busy people or for those who live outside the area. In these situations, the title company or attorney emails or express mails the appropriate documents to the seller and buyer. This is particularly easy for cash deals; in most of these cases, the buyer simply needs to sign the closing statement, and email or fax it back to the sender. If a mortgage loan is involved, the lender requires a copy with blue-ink signatures, so the loan documents must be mailed back.

The mail-away situation is a little more complicated for sellers because they must sign the deed in front of a U.S. approved notary. While it's usually easy to find a notary in the U.S., it may be more difficult to find one in a foreign country. International banks and U.S. embassies should have a notary available, but in some countries, the seller may have to travel quite a distance to reach such a facility. Alternatively, the seller may be able to find an attorney who does business with the U.S.; be prepared to pay hundreds of dollars for a notary's services if this is the chosen option.

Another alternative to attending a closing is to authorize someone to attend and sign the documents for you. Real estate agents sometimes agree to do this for their clients. In order to legally sign for someone, the signing party must have a power of attorney authorization. The closing agent can supply the preferred form that must be signed by the buyer or seller in front of a U.S. approved notary.

This concludes the 100 tips that the author believes will be a useful addition to any current or future property owner's library. Visit http://amazon.com/author/patriciaoconnor to view Patricia O'Connor's other published books.

www.ingramcontent.com/pod-product-compliance
Lightning Source LLC
Chambersburg PA
CBHW051330170526
45166CB00002B/748